The Civil War

SLAVERY AND THE CIVIL WAR

Linda R. Wade

ABDO
Daughters Publishing

Visit us at
www.abdopub.com

Graphic Design: John Hamilton
Contributing Editors: John Hamilton; Alan Gergen; Elizabeth Clouter-Gergen
Cover photo: John Hamilton; Digital Stock
Interior photos: Archive Photos, page 15; Corbis-Bettmann, pages 7, 9, 10, 13,
14, 22, 25; Digital Stock, pages 1, 5, 19
Illustration: John Hamilton, page 17

Sources: Barges, Eric Wonderwork. *The War Between the States.* New York:
McGraw-Hill Book Co., 1959; Jordan, Robert P. *The Civil War.* Washington,
D.C.: National Geographic Society, 1969; Kallen, Stuart A. *Days of Slavery.*
Edina, Minnesota: Abdo & Daughters Publishing, 1990; McClard, Megan.
Harriet Tubman: Slavery and the Underground Railroad. Englewood Cliffs, N.J.:
Silver Burdett Press, 1991; Ray, Delia. *Behind the Blue and the Gray.* New York:
Lodestar Books, 1991; Ray, Delia. *A Nation Torn: The Story of How the Civil
War Began.* New York: Lodestar Books, 1990; Reger, James P. *Life in the North
During the Civil War.* San Diego, CA: Lucent Books, 1997; Reger, James P. *Life
in the South During the Civil War.* San Diego, CA: Lucent Books, 1997; Sandler,
Martin W. *Civil War.* New York: HarperCollins Publishers, 1996; Shumate, Jane.
Sojourner Truth and the Voice of Freedom. Brookfield, Connecticut: The
Millbrook Press, 1991.

Library of Congress Cataloging–in–Publication Data

Wade, Linda R.
    Slavery and the Civil War / Linda Wade
        p. cm. — (The Civil War)
    Includes index.
    Summary: Examines the issues leading up to the Civil War, its primary causes,
principal figures, reasons for the secession of the South, first battle, and the
effects of such acts as the Missouri Compromise and Kansas-Nebraska Act.
    ISBN 1-56239-826-1
    1. United States—History—Civil War, 1861-1865—Causes.
[1. United States—History—Civil War, 1861-1865.] I. Title. II. Series: Wade,
Linda R., Civil War.
E459.W24 1998
973.7' 11—dc21   97-37478
                                                          CIP
                                                           AC

CONTENTS

Introduction 4

Early Problems 6

Changes of the 1850s 10

The Antislavery Movement 12

A Nation Divided 16

Acts and Compromises 18

Changes in the Political System 21

Abraham Lincoln for President 24

Early Days of the Lincoln Presidency 27

Internet Sites 29

Glossary 30

Index 32

INTRODUCTION

When we hear the words, *Civil War*, certain images come to mind. The first is, probably, *slavery*. Congress could not find an agreeable answer to this problem. Each new act and decision seemed to make matters worse. Working conditions in both the North and South were hard. The economy was sliding. The country was growing so fast that it could not meet the needs of its people.

Before solutions could be found, the first shot was fired. Between 1861 and 1865, more than three million men fought on many battlefields. Churches and farms sheltered the dying. Homes became headquarters. Armies marched across farms. Americans killed Americans. Brothers wearing opposite uniforms met on the battlefield. A divided nation found itself facing circumstances where families were torn apart.

The Civil War began as a bitter dispute over Union and States' Rights. It ended as a struggle over the meaning of freedom in America.

What many thought would be a short uprising became an agonizing four-year war. A nation was split. How did this happen?

Facing page: Former slave Frederick Douglass helped lead the abolitionist movement.

CHAPTER 1

EARLY PROBLEMS

Historians have long debated the causes of the Civil War. Some thought conflicts over borders, freedom, and tariffs were early problems. Others believed the varied lifestyles in the North and South led to the war. In 1800, only eight million people lived in America. However, by 1861, the number of Americans had risen to 31 million. States and territories had been added. Railroads tied the East to the western edges of civilization. Travel was now much easier, and news moved faster.

Problems arose as settlers established homes. As more people settled in the North, industry became the chief source of income. Factories were built. Many farmers left their farms and moved to the cities. Boat docks were busy with the loading and unloading of goods moving between Europe and the United States. These early times gave birth to free labor, which meant that people began to choose for themselves where and for whom to work.

During the mid-1800s, millions of men and women from foreign countries came to America. They sought a better life. Across the world, news had spread of the job opportunities in this new land. Men sought work in the mills and factories of the North.

It was different in the South. While the North became more industrialized, the South remained rural. There were few cities with factories. Only small towns dotted the countryside. Early settlers had found the climate warm and perfect for farming.

The farm was the center of most of the activity in the South. As the farmers prospered, they cleared more and more land in order to plant more crops. These large farms were called plantations. As a result, the South's chief source of income became large-scale farming.

Cotton was the main crop, especially after the cotton gin was invented in 1793. The cotton gin was used to remove seeds from cotton fibers. Before its invention by Eli Whitney, slaves removed seeds by hand. Ordinarily, it took a slave 10 hours to pull the seeds from just one pound (.45 kg) of cotton. With the cotton gin, 1,000 pounds (450 kg) of clean fiber could be produced each day. Now farmers planted cotton on every available patch of ground. Tobacco and sugar cane were also important crops grown in the South.

In order for the plantation owners to produce the needed crops, they used slave labor. Slave labor was when a person was purchased and forced to work without choice. Many black people were bought and sold as slaves. They were forced to serve their masters both in

A cotton plantation on the shores of the Mississippi River.

and out of the plantation home. They did most of the cooking, cleaning, and household duties.

In the beginning, most Southern farmers were too poor to use slave labor. As these farms grew and became large plantations, the white owners bought more and more slaves to plant and harvest their crops. These rich fields in the South provided the raw materials necessary to the factories and mills of the North.

Even England was requesting cotton and products from the South. There seemed no end to the need for raw material. To feed this need, more slaves were bought and used in the fields.

Slavery was not a new thing. Some people pretended it did not exist. Others spoke out against it. It was often debated in Congress.

Slave trade had become an issue in colonial days. During the 1680s, Quakers in Pennsylvania spoke against slavery on moral grounds. In the late 1700s, several leaders of the American revolutionary movement spoke out against slavery as well.

In 1787, lawmakers in Congress had an important debate. They tried to decide how to choose the number of representatives a state could send to Washington, D.C. Should slaves be counted as part of the population? They decided that since slaves were not considered citizens, only three-fifths of a state's total number of slaves could be counted. This was called the Three-Fifths Compromise.

There was also a debate over foreign slave trade. Northern states wanted Congress to have the power to forbid this trade. Southern delegates did not want Congress to have this power. The compromise decided that Congress would not be allowed to regulate the foreign slave trade until 1808.

As the country grew and territories wished to become states, the Southern plantation owners looked westward to expand their way of life.

An American slave market.

In 1820, Henry Clay, a representative from Kentucky, helped write the Missouri Compromise. To please the South it permitted slavery in the new state of Missouri. However, Maine would be a free state. The compromise also prohibited slavery in the Louisiana Territory.

The country was at peace for almost 30 years. Then in the spring of 1846, war broke out with Mexico. The United States declared victory two years later. As a result of the war, America gained nearly one million square miles (2.5 million square km) of new territories in the Southwest.

About this same time, songs of Stephen Foster filled the air. He wrote toe-tappers like "Camptown Races" and "Oh! Susannah." But he also wrote the sentimental favorites "My Old Kentucky Home" and "Jeanie with the Light Brown Hair." His songs provided a soft, gentle, and attractive view of black people in the South.

CHAPTER 2

CHANGES OF THE 1850s

In Washington, D.C., slavery continued to be a big issue for the new states and territories. Should these states be free or slave states?

Henry Clay, now a senator, was called the Great Compromiser. He had written the Missouri Compromise. Now he needed to find a new answer that would satisfy both North and South. He found the solution in the Compromise of 1850. These acts authorized abolition of slavery in the District of Columbia (of which the cities of Washington and Georgetown were a part), and declared that California would be admitted as a free state.

The Compromise also included a strict Fugitive Slave Act. Clay included this act to satisfy the South. It said Northerners were required to return escaped slaves to their Southern owners. Many people of the North ignored the law. Some were actually willing to help slaves escape to freedom. But when they promoted antislavery activities, they were called abolitionists.

Southerners resented the abolitionists. They feared that the speeches of these radicals would stir up their slaves. They remembered when in the summer of 1831, Nat Turner, a Virginia slave, led 70 black followers in a brutal revolt. During their bloody march from farm to farm, the slaves murdered 55 whites. This rebellion left Southerners afraid for their lives.

The Southern states reacted quickly. They wanted to keep the abolitionist movement from making any more trouble. Laws limiting the freedom of speech and press were passed. Newspapers owned by the abolitionists were burned. Plantation owners closely watched their slaves.

Now there were tighter restrictions on the growth of slavery, and the South felt threatened. In 1850, Senator John C. Calhoun of South Carolina warned in a speech on the Senate floor: "I have. . . believed from the first that the agitation of the subject of slavery would, if not prevented by some timely and effective measure, end in disunion. . ."

During the same year, the abolitionists developed the Underground Railroad. This was a system by which escaped slaves were fed and housed while traveling north. The routes led from the slave states to the free states and Canada. Between 1850 and 1860, around 20,000 slaves used this way to escape.

Facing page: Runaway slaves arriving at Leon Coffin's Indiana farm, a busy station of the Underground Railroad.

CHAPTER 3

THE ANTISLAVERY MOVEMENT

Harriet Tubman was known for her Underground Railroad activities. The blacks called her Moses because she led them to freedom. She was born a slave but escaped in 1849. She went to Philadelphia, Pennsylvania, by way of the Underground Railroad. She returned to the South 18 times to help hundreds of slaves flee from their cruel masters. On one of her last trips north, she helped her parents to freedom. Rewards for her capture went up to $40,000, but she was never caught. None of the slaves she was helping to escape were caught either.

Harriet Beecher Stowe also played a role in antislavery. She wrote the book, *Uncle Tom's Cabin*. Her writing revealed the terrible picture of slavery as it really was in the South. She exposed the way that slave families were sold separately. She told how the slave masters would beat their slaves. She showed how dogs were used to chase and bring down any escaping slave. The Southerners were angry at what she said. Northerners became more active in speaking out against slavery.

Born a slave, Harriet Tubman led escaped slaves to freedom on the Underground Railroad.

Author Harriet Beecher Stowe.

Another black woman spoke out against slavery. Her name was Sojourner Truth. She had been born a slave in New York. Her name then was Isabella. She received her freedom when slavery was banned in 1843. She began making speeches against slavery. Her strong voice stirred the people. She told them what slavery was all about. She led people and moved them to action.

Frederick Douglass was also a former slave who told people about slavery. He was born on a Maryland plantation. When he was about seven years old, he learned to read and write. This made his master angry. Douglass decided that education must be important. As he read and learned what was happening, he knew he must help his people. When he was 20, he escaped to Massachusetts.

Douglass began attending antislavery meetings. He began to speak out. He wrote articles for the newspapers. He also helped about 400 Southern slaves escape slavery.

The issue of slavery was getting bigger by the minute. It was the topic of conversations in every meeting place. People looked to the leaders and to Congress for an answer.

An advertisement for Stowe's antislavery novel, *Uncle Tom's Cabin*.

A NATION DIVIDED

SLAVERY AND THE CIVIL WAR

Harriet Tubman escaped slavery in 1849. She was very active in the Underground Railroad, helping hundreds of slaves escape to the North. She was nicknamed "Moses" because she led so many of her people to freedom.

Uncle Tom's Cabin, by Harriet Beecher Stowe, was published in 1852. It showed the cruelty of slavery, and sold more than 300,000 copies in its first year.

Frederick Douglass was a former slave who learned to read and write, then used his education to teach people about the evils of slavery. He spoke at antislavery rallies, wrote newspaper articles, and helped about 400 slaves escape to freedom.

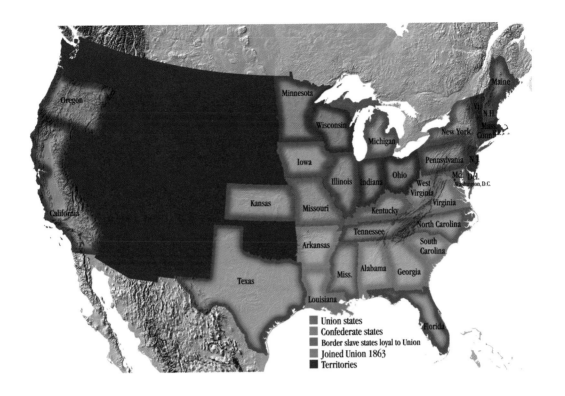

Union states
Confederate states
Border slave states loyal to Union
Joined Union 1863
Territories

On October 16, 1859, abolitionist John Brown captured the federal armory at Harpers Ferry, Virginia. His capture and hanging hardened both sides of the slavery issue.

Abraham Lincoln called slavery the "cancer" of bondage. His election as president in 1860 threatened the white establishment in the South. Within a few months, the Confederacy was formed, and the Civil War had begun.

CHAPTER 4

ACTS AND COMPROMISES

Congress made another attempt to solve the problem. The Kansas-Nebraska Act was written in 1854. It repealed the Missouri Compromise. It also dealt with the problem of slavery in the new regions. The Kansas and Nebraska Territories would allow slavery. However, when they became states, the people would vote whether to continue slavery or become a free state. This was called popular sovereignty. Many Northerners opposed the act. They feared that once slavery was in a territory, it was there to stay.

The act was tested when, in 1861, Kansas voted to be a free state. Settlers who strongly favored slavery and settlers who hated slavery had both rushed to Kansas. During the next 10 years, fighting broke out many times. More than 200 men were killed. The state was often called "Bleeding Kansas."

Violence also erupted as far away as Washington, D.C. Preston Brooks was a proslavery representative from South Carolina. He beat antislavery Senator Charles Sumner of Massachusetts on the head with a walking cane. Sumner had made an antislavery speech.

Newspapers told of the beating. Southerner sympathizers sent Brooks canes to show their support. However, when one man heard about it, he was ready to strike back. His name was John Brown. He was an abolitionist from Massachusetts. He had also been a part of

Abolitionist John Brown.

the Underground Railroad. Then he went to Kansas in order to fight slavery there.

After hearing the news, Brown and his band of 21 free-state guerrillas headed east. For a while they lived in Maryland. He planned to capture guns from a place called Harpers Ferry. This little town was located where the Shenandoah and Potomac Rivers met in Virginia (later West Virginia). He needed these weapons to start a slave rebellion.

On Sunday, October 16, 1859, Brown made his attack. They captured the federal weapons. As news went out, he expected slaves from nearby plantations to join him. However, they were too afraid of the consequences. John Brown was trapped.

President James Buchanan sent a group of marines, led by Colonel Robert E. Lee, to capture Brown and the fort. Two of Brown's sons were killed in the attack. Brown was slashed by a marine's sword. Still badly wounded, he was brought to trial. Brown said, "If it be deemed necessary that I should forfeit my life for the furtherance of the ends of justice, and mingle my blood further with the blood of my children and with the blood of millions in this slave country whose rights are disregarded by wicked, cruel, and unjust enactments—I submit. So let it be done."

John Brown was hanged on December 2, 1859, six weeks after the raid. The South was glad he was gone, for he stood for Northern aggressiveness.

The scene was different in the North. They mourned his death. He became a martyr. Harriet Tubman considered him to be the true liberator of black people. The John Brown incident was the beginning of the Confederate army.

CHAPTER 5

CHANGES IN THE POLITICAL SYSTEM

Changes were occurring every day. The Kansas-Nebraska Act so stirred the country that it changed the political party system. The Republican Party was formed in 1854. This group opposed slavery and its growth into the new territories and states. The two largest political parties at that time were the Whigs and the Democrats.

In 1857, the Supreme Court of the United States tried to settle the slavery issue with its Dred Scott Decision. Scott was a slave who claimed freedom because he had lived for a time in a free state and territory. The court said that a slave, being property, had no constitutional rights as a citizen. It further ruled that Congress could not prohibit slavery in the new territories.

The ruling exploded like fireworks throughout the nation. The South was happy to have its arguments upheld. The North denounced the Court and said it was working for the South. One thing was sure: neither Congress nor the Supreme Court could settle the conflict over slavery.

During the time that all these things were happening, two men were shaping the future of the country. Stephen A. Douglas was a senator from Illinois. He had introduced the Kansas-Nebraska Act. He refused to admit that slavery was wrong.

A beardless Abraham Lincoln at about the time of the Lincoln-Douglas Debates.

His Republican opponent was named Abraham Lincoln. He called slavery the "cancer" of bondage. He also said that the Dred Scott case had opened the way for slavery to enter all the territories. Lincoln thought that the Union would stay together, but that it would become all slave or all free.

These two men not only had opposing ideas, but they also looked very different. Douglas was short and had a large round head. Some said he looked like a fierce bulldog. They called him "Little Giant." His voice boomed out at the audience. He always appeared in fancy clothes and rode the best horses.

On the other hand, Lincoln was a tall man. He looked awkward and his clothes seemed loose. His voice was high and calm and people seemed to hear him better. They called him the "Railsplitter." Sometimes he was called "Long Abe." He was a simple man and often slipped into his seat unnoticed.

Lincoln's campaign advisers knew that Douglas drew large crowds when he gave speeches. They decided to have Lincoln follow Douglas and then speak to the same people. Douglas traveled by train. As the train approached, a cannon boomed out. People came to hear him talk.

Often in the same passenger train Lincoln sat quietly until after Douglas had talked to the people. Then he spoke to them about how he wanted to bring the nation together.

Douglas was angry that Lincoln was following him. So Lincoln changed his tactics. He challenged Douglas to a series of debates. They would discuss the issues face to face and let the people decide for themselves.

CHAPTER 6

ABRAHAM LINCOLN FOR PRESIDENT

Seven dates were set for the Lincoln-Douglas Debates. The candidates would debate the extension of slavery into free territory. These debates attracted national attention. Crowds came to listen and cheer them. They waved banners. People enjoyed the festive atmosphere. Reporters followed these men everywhere they went. The newspapers were filled with their remarks.

Finally, the time came to choose the Illinois senator. It was a close election, but Abraham Lincoln lost. He had campaigned four long months and was disappointed at the loss. He told his friends, "I am too big to cry and too badly hurt to laugh."

Lincoln made a good impression on the Illinois Republican newspaper reporters. They began talking about him as a presidential candidate.

Meanwhile, he went back to his law practice in Springfield. Political figures came to visit him. They wanted to know his views. Republican groups invited him to give speeches. After the John Brown incident, he encouraged his fellow Republicans to do their part to preserve peace and harmony throughout the country.

In May of 1860, the Republicans held their national convention in Chicago, Illinois. Lincoln followers crowded into the hall. It took three days, but finally four delegates from Ohio changed their vote.

Abraham Lincoln at the Lincoln-Douglas Debates.

They made Abraham Lincoln a candidate for president of the United States.

The Democrats had met a few weeks before. There were serious disagreements. They argued about slaveholders, slaves, and federal laws. The arguments were so strong that 50 Southern Democrats walked out of the Charleston, Virginia, convention.

Then the Democrats broke into two different wings. The Northern Democrats met in Baltimore, Maryland. They nominated Stephen A. Douglas for president. Southern Democrats went to Richmond, Virginia. They chose John C. Breckinridge of Kentucky to be their candidate.

With a broken Democratic party, a Republican victory appeared sure. Even Douglas realized his chances for winning were slim. He simply campaigned for national unity.

To the South, the election became a threat to their way of life. Lincoln ran on the platform of halting the further spread of slavery. He said, "Those who deny freedom to others deserve it not for themselves and under a just God cannot retain it." The Southerners thought they would lose what they called "their property." Without the slaves, they faced ruin. Without slave labor, there would be no crops and no money.

Soon it was November 6, 1860—Election Day. People were anxious to vote. Still, Lincoln was uncertain. He knew he was not even on the ballot in 10 Southern states. So he watched and listened to the telegraph lines.

Finally, the news came. Abraham Lincoln had won the election. He would be the sixteenth president of the United States. Northerners were happy. The South mourned. The Augusta, Georgia *Constitution* said, "The South should arm at once." Other Southern newspapers carried the news with a black border. It was a death notice to them.

What was going to happen?

CHAPTER 7

EARLY DAYS OF THE LINCOLN PRESIDENCY

Abraham Lincoln knew it would not be easy to be the president. Just before the election, Southerners said that a Republican victory would mean disunion. Southern leaders had been threatening to withdraw from the Union for years. No one thought they were serious.

But the die had been cast.

On December 20, just a few weeks after the election, South Carolina seceded, breaking away from the rest of the country. Delegates from across the state met in Charleston and voted unanimously to establish an independent nation. It would allow for the right to own slaves. In January, five other Southern states rushed to leave the Union. Those states were Mississippi, Florida, Alabama, Georgia, and Louisiana.

In February, representatives from these states met in Montgomery, Alabama. They established the Confederate States of America. Jefferson Davis, a senator from Mississippi, was chosen to be their president. He opposed Steven Douglas' Freeport Doctrine. This idea said that the people of a territory could exclude slavery by refusing to protect it. The South became the Confederacy.

Lincoln continued to read all the newspapers. He received telegrams and letters. He knew the country was in great stress. What could he do to bring Americans together? He struggled with this as he wrote his inauguration speech.

A week before he became president, Lincoln traveled to Washington, D.C. He spoke to crowds all along the way. There were rumors that assassins wanted to kill him. But he arrived safely. Stephen A. Douglas was there to meet him. He pledged support to his old friend and rival.

In March, Texas joined the Confederacy. Even Virginia, birthplace of seven presidents, seemed sure to follow.

Two days later, Abraham Lincoln was sworn in as president. He declared, "We will do all in our power to preserve the Union."

War talk could be heard everywhere. Fear filled the air. Volunteers wanted to do their part. Recruits were anxious to join the army and help settle what they thought would be a "little uprising." No one thought the "war" would last more than a "couple of weeks, maybe a month." Many of these young men had never fired a gun in battle or lived outdoors. For others, hard times in the North meant that work was hard to get. As a volunteer soldier, a private could make $13 a month. The army also offered excitement and adventure. Many men had never traveled past their own hometowns.

Soon, many would not only leave their homes, but also they would die. The Union and Confederate armies would meet many times. Their first encounter would happen soon at Fort Sumter. War would take on new meaning.

INTERNET SITES

Civil War Forum
AOL keyword: Civil War

This comprehensive site on America Online is a great place to start learning more about the Civil War. The forum is divided into four main groups. In the "Mason-Dixon Line Chat Room" you can interact with fellow Civil War buffs. The "Civil War Information Center" is especially good for historians and reenactors, and includes help with tracking down your Civil War ancestors. The "Civil War Archive" is full of downloadable text and graphic files, including old photos from the National Archives. When you're ready for more in-depth information, the "Civil War Internet" group provides many links to other sites.

The United States Civil War Center
http://www.cwc.lsu.edu/civlink.htm

This is a very extensive index of Civil War information available on the Internet, including archives and special collections, biographies, famous battlefields, books and films, maps, newspapers, and just about everything you would want to find on the Civil War. The site currently has over 1,800 web links.

These sites are subject to change. Go to your favorite search engine and type in "Civil War" for more sites.

PASS IT ON

Civil War buffs: educate readers around the country by passing on interesting information you've learned about the Civil War. Maybe your family visited a famous Civil War battle site, or you've taken part in a reenactment. Who's your favorite historical figure from the Civil War? We want to hear from you!

To get posted on the ABDO & Daughters website, E-mail us at "History@abdopub.com"

Visit the ABDO & Daughters website at www.abdopub.com

GLOSSARY

Abolitionist

Radical Northerners who promoted antislavery activities.

Compromise of 1850

Laws passed by Congress in 1850 allowing California to enter the Union as a free state, and authorizing the abolition of slavery in the District of Columbia, which included the cities of Washington and Georgetown. The compromise also strengthened laws requiring runaway slaves to be returned to their Southern masters.

Confederate Army

Southern army.

Confederate States of America

Eleven states that withdrew from the United States in 1860-1861. These included: Alabama, Arkansas, Florida, Georgia, Louisiana, Mississippi, North Carolina, South Carolina, Tennessee, Texas, and Virginia.

Cotton Gin

Machine invented by Eli Whitney to remove seeds from cotton fibers.

Free Labor

When people are free to choose their place of employment.

Fugitive Slave Act

Act passed by Congress as part of the Compromise of 1850, which required Northerners to return escaped slaves to their Southern owners.

Kansas-Nebraska Act

A law written in 1854 to repeal the Missouri Compromise and deal with the problem of slavery in the new regions.

Missouri Compromise

Bill passed by Congress in 1820 that permitted slavery in the new state of Missouri. It said that Maine would be a free state. It also said that slavery would not be permitted in the Louisiana Territory.

Plantation

A large farm found in the South that used slave labor.

Popular Sovereignty

The people choose to continue slavery or become a free state.

Secede

Withdraw from the United States.

Slave Labor

When a person is forced to work without the choice of who he or she is working for, or the kind of work that person is doing.

Three-Fifths Compromise

A congressional statement that said only three-fifths of a state's total number of slaves could be counted when determining the number of representatives.

Underground Railroad

Imaginary railway used by slaves to escape.

Union

Another name for the United States. Twenty four states remained loyal to the Union during the Civil War.

Union Army

Northern army.

White Flag

A sign of surrender.

INDEX

A
abolitionist 11, 16
Alabama 27
Augusta, Georgia 26

B
Baltimore, Maryland 26
Breckinridge, John C. 26
Brooks, Preston 16
Brown, John 9, 16, 20, 24
Buchanan, James 20

C
Calhoun, John C. 11
California 10
Canada 11
Charleston, Virginia 26
Chicago, Illinois 24
Clay, Henry 9, 10
Compromise of 1850 10
Confederacy 20, 27, 28
Confederate Army 20
Confederate States of
      America 27
Congress, United States
      4, 8, 15, 16, 21
cotton 7, 8
cotton gin 7

D
Davis, Jefferson 27
Democrat 21, 26
Douglas, Stephen A. 21,
      23, 24, 26, 28
Douglass, Frederick 15
Dred Scott Decision 21

E
England 8

F
Florida 27
Fort Sumter 28
Foster, Stephen 9
Free Labor 6
Free-State guerrillas 20

Freeport Doctrine 27
Fugitive Slave Act 10

G
Georgia 26, 27

H
Harpers Ferry 20

I
Illinois 21, 24

K
Kansas 16, 21
Kansas-Nebraska
      Act 16, 21
Kentucky 9, 26

L
Lee, Robert E. 20
Lincoln, Abraham 23, 24,
      26, 27, 28
Lincoln-Douglas Debates
      24
Louisiana 9, 27

M
Maine 9
Maryland 15, 20, 26
Massachusetts 15, 16
Mexico 9
Mississippi 27
Missouri Compromise 9,
      10, 16
Montgomery, Alabama 27
Moses 12

N
Nebraska 16, 21

O
Ohio 24

P
Pennsylvania 8, 12
Philadelphia, Pennsylvania
      12

plantation 7, 8, 11, 15, 20

Q
Quakers 8

R
railroads 6
Republican 21, 24, 26, 27
Richmond, Virginia 26

S
Scott, Dred 21, 23
United States Senate 11
slave labor 7, 8, 26
South Carolina 11, 16, 27
Springfield, Illinois 24
Stowe, Harriet Beecher 12
sugar cane 7
Sumner, Charles 16
United States Supreme
      Court 21

T
Texas 28
Three-Fifths Compromise
      8
tobacco 7
Truth, Sojourner 15
Tubman, Harriet 12, 20
Turner, Nat 11

U
Uncle Tom's Cabin 12
Underground Railroad 11,
      12, 16
Union 4, 23, 27, 28

V
Virginia 11, 20, 26, 28

W
Washington, D.C. 8, 10,
      16, 28
West Virginia 20
Whig 21
Whitney, Eli 7